LAWS OF EXPANSION

Richard Ciaramitaro

Belleville, Ontario, Canada

Laws of Expansion
Copyright © 2001, Richard Ciaramitaro

All Scripture quotations, unless otherwise specified, are from *The Holy Bible, King James Version*. Copyright © 1977, 1984, Thomas Nelson Inc., Publishers.

Laws of Expansion was produced from an audio tape transcript of a series of messages preached by Pastor Richard Ciaramitaro at Windsor Christian Fellowship in 1996. Although the material has been edited for use in this book, it nevertheless continues to reflect Pastor Rick's unique oral style and should be read with this in mind.

ISBN: 1-55306-261-2

Essence Publishing is a Christian Book Publisher dedicated to furthering the work of Christ through the written word. *Guardian Books* is an imprint of *Essence Publishing*. For more information, contact:
44 Moira Street West, Belleville, Ontario, Canada K8P 1S3.
Phone: 1-800-238-6376. Fax: (613) 962-3055.
E-mail: info@essencegroup.com
Internet: www.essencegroup.com

Printed in Canada
by
Guardian BOOKS

*I dedicate this book to
my Lord and Saviour Jesus Christ,
who desires to do "exceeding abundantly
above all that we ask or think,
according to the power that worketh in us"*
(Eph. 3:20).

Contents

Acknowledgements

A note of thanks to the following individuals:

To my Board and Eldership, who have seen our church through with their prayer and support during times of transition.

To Nello Paolini, for being "mellow" in stretching times.

To my wife, Cathy, who encourages me to launch out into the deep.

To Akin Taiwo and my son-in-law, Mike Mendler, for producing and editing the transcripts.

To the Holy Spirit, who has taken me through each of the steps outlined in this book and has been so faithful, gracious and longsuffering with me along the way.

And most of all, to my Lord Jesus, who gives us all the grace to reach for, and fulfill, the High Calling of God for our lives.

ONE

Introduction

God is building His Church. Psalm 127:1 says, *"Except the LORD build the house, they labour in vain that build it."* But as this Scripture suggests, God doesn't work alone. He uses men full of the Holy Spirit to get the job done. Needs are met only as each person actively does his or her part.

I shared this truth with our church congregation almost seventeen years ago and God has brought us a long way from our humble beginnings. We started off with a budget of about $500 per week. Then we moved up to $2,000. Then, to over $30,000 per week. Today, our yearly budget is in the millions; we have over sixty employees on staff, and God is continuing to move us forward.

My conviction, then and now, is that God's resources are unlimited. He made all things and He owns everything, but if we wish to see our visions come to pass we must learn to cooperate with His *laws of expansion*. These laws, as outlined in Isaiah 54, are the subject of this book. It is my sincere prayer that as you read this book, the Lord will open the eyes of your understanding so that you may grasp the fullness of all that He's prepared for you, and help you to master the principles of expansion—to the praise of His glory.

For the Visionary

I believe that I am a man with a vision. God has given me a vision for our local church, for the corporate church in our city and for the city itself. Reverend James Beale, the long-time pastor of Bethesda Christian Church in Sterling Heights, MI, is a man I greatly respect in ministry. He once came to our church for the dedication of one of our church building phases. During his visit, he remarked that whoever would do what we were endeavouring to do must be a visionary, and must also have an ability from God to persuade others to pay for that vision. He was right.

Having a vision is actually a necessary and godly requirement. The Word of God tells us that where there is no vision, the people perish (Prov. 29:18). It is God's desire that we learn to see things before they actually happen. Jesus saw Calvary and the grave long before he was there. He also saw the resurrection, the ascension and the redeemed Church. He even prophesied about the days we are presently living in. His vision of what lay ahead gave Him the momentum to go to the cross and die for us.

God showed Noah His plan for the ark, and Noah laboured perhaps a hundred years to see the vision fulfilled. Joseph had a dream that he would one day be a ruler, and although it went unfulfilled for twenty-two years, that vision sustained him through extraordinary trials. But in due time, God promoted him, and Joseph went from the prison to the palace—from prison inmate to governor of the land of Egypt in a single day. That was *expansion*.

Vision and expansion are closely related. Unless you are a visionary—or desire to be one—expansion is for you a non-issue. Why expand when you are content to stay where you are?

What is Expansion?

To expand something is to increase the extent of it. It is to increase the number or scope of that thing. According to Webster's dictionary, the word *expand* also means to feel generous or optimistic.[1] To be optimistic is to have a high spirit and a positive outlook. You can't expand your business if you don't have a positive outlook about it. Optimism and enthusiasm are godly characteristics. Consequently, they are also powerful spiritual forces.

To expand also means to "swell." If your foot swells up, it goes beyond its original limit. It is beyond normal—whatever normal is for you.

Another shade of meaning of the word *expand* is to "distend." The implication is of *pressure from within forcing extension outward*. That's exactly what happened in Jerusalem in Acts 8. Jesus had already told the disciples to bring the gospel beyond the borders of Jerusalem, but it didn't happen until He allowed pressure—in this case, persecution—to be exerted on the early Church. Then, as they fled into the surrounding regions, they spread the good news along the way!

The New Testament, as well as the Old, teaches that it is God's will for His people to experience increase in their lives:

And the Lord make you to increase and abound in love one toward another, and toward all men, even as we do toward you (1 Thess. 3:12).

The preceding Scripture tells us that God desires us to increase in love toward one another. This is the first and most important area of increase, but there are many others. As we will see, God's desire is that we would expand in many ways for the purpose of bringing glory to His Name.

What Motivates You?

The Bible calls us a unique or "peculiar" people (1 Pet. 2;9). In other words, God wants us to be different. We're not to be fitted into the world's mold or way. We shouldn't conform to its norms and expectations and empty traditions (Rom. 12:2). Nor should our motivation be worldly. On the contrary, our driving energy and motivating force is the Holy Ghost, who moves us to do things that are pleasing to our heavenly Father.

Money drives some people. Fear drives some others. But we are to be motivated by the things of the Spirit (Rom. 7:6). Our purpose in life is to please and exalt God— not ourselves or other men. Our purpose in life is to be great in the Kingdom, which means to be a servant—not the served one. When we are so motivated, we will see God's Kingdom expand in our day and hour.

Expansion is usually preceded by a high spirit, coupled with a benevolent inclination toward others. In other words, there will be a high level of morale among believers and a readiness to be motivated by the Holy Spirit to fulfill God's requirements. A right motivation frees God to work His utmost in and through you.

Laws of Expansion

It is significant that the five laws of expansion outlined in Isaiah 54:2 are preceded by the words *"Sing, O barren, thou that didst not bear; break forth into singing..."* (Isa. 54:1). A barren person is an unfruitful person. Barren people are often sorrowful people. It's no fun to see no results for your labour—no matter what it is you're labouring for. Why, then, would God instruct an unfruitful person to sing? Because God was revealing a supernatural principle here—a wonderful promise for the unfruitful that is cause for rejoicing. In this verse, God was speaking prophetically about the Church. You see, God had come to the nation of Israel in the Old Testament time and revealed Himself in a powerful way—but they didn't receive Him. As a result, God was announcing through the prophet Isaiah that He was about to reveal Himself to the Gentiles, who at that time weren't producing any fruit for God because they were outsiders and strangers to God's covenants (Eph. 2:12). Today, however, the Gentiles are producing more fruit for the Kingdom than their Jewish predecessors—just as the promise predicted.

But the good news is that this promise applies not only to the corporate Church, but to you personally. Are you barren today? Have you laboured for something in the Kingdom only to come up empty-handed? Are there areas in your life that resemble a barren womb? If so, rejoice! God has targeted you for expansion.

How does one go about realizing this expansion? The five laws (or prerequisites) of expansion are contained in Isaiah 54:2:

Enlarge the place of thy tent, and let them stretch forth the curtains of thine habitations: spare not, lengthen thy cords, and strengthen thy stakes.

Severally, they include:

1. Enlarge the place of thy tent
2. Stretch forth the curtains
3. Spare not
4. Lengthen thy cords
5. Strengthen thy stakes

If you faithfully fulfill all of these laws, you will experience the outcome described in verse three:

For thou shalt break forth on the right hand and on the left; and thy seed shall inherit the Gentiles and make the desolate cities to be inhabited.

God will touch the barren areas of your life and cause them to be fruitful. The hand of His favour on your life will be evident. He will even cause your children to bring salvation to the nations.

And as if that weren't enough, this promise is followed up by another in verse four:

Fear not; for thou shalt not be ashamed: neither be thou confounded; for thou shalt not be put to shame: for thou shalt forget the shame of thy youth and shalt not remember the reproach of thy widowhood any more.

In other words, you will not be frustrated or put to shame, for God will see to it that his purposes for your life are fulfilled.

Would you like to see our succeeding generations do great things for God? They will if we learn to fulfill and then teach them His laws of expansion. Our offspring will inherit the nations. We will see the desolate places of the earth where there has been no move of God become the habitation of God's presence.

TWO

Enlarge

"Enlarge the place of thy tent..." (Isa. 54:2).

The first law of expansion is to *enlarge*. *"Enlarge the place of thy tent,"* God said through His prophet. To enlarge means to broaden, make room, widen, magnify or amplify. "Enlarge the scope of your vision," God is saying. Have a mentality change, and expand the horizons of possibility. The truth be known, God's people aren't to think "normally." Rather, we're to think *supernaturally* because we have the mind of Christ (1 Cor. 2:16). We should not allow the world to impose limitations on what we think because we live in a higher realm.

Whenever God speaks to me about something, I don't try to think it through anymore. I don't even attempt to figure it out. Does that mean I put my brain on hold? Not in any way. The Bible says we should trust in the Lord with all of our hearts and not lean on (or be limited by) our understanding (Prov. 3:5). That means we should not allow the tendencies of ours minds to dictate our actions.

The Bible is full of things that defy our understanding. I can't understand the virgin birth. I can't understand why God would tell a whole army to walk around Jericho seven times. I can't understand why Jesus spit on the sand to heal a blind man. The Old Testament prophets didn't understand everything God showed them or told them to do either, but they were nevertheless extremely effective in their service for God. If we're determined to figure everything out we'll probably do nothing. Let it be enough for us to know that God has a plan and that plan is unfolding on the earth today. Let's allow God to change the way we operate.

If you are to enlarge, your focus needs to be on God, because only He has the ability to make you realize the possibilities and dreams He's deposited in your heart.

What is the size of your household and city? God wants to extend His hands through you to them. My own city has over 200,000 individuals who must be reached by the gospel of Christ. Why? Because God is concerned about them. The task is too great for one church alone; only the corporate Body of Christ in our city has the ability to do that, with each member in each church doing his or her part. But the first step in the process is to "enlarge the tent," to enlarge our vision beyond the scope of our personal goals and church agendas, to develop the mentality or vision to see the job accomplished.

But having the mentality or vision is just the start, of course. We must also work toward achieving the vision. Suppose we've been afraid to share the gospel? Nobody will come to the light of Christ. Suppose we've been timid about our faith? Nobody will know of the power of God to save and deliver. God wants us to expand and to enlarge the place of our tent. He wants us to reach out to others and bring them into His fold. He wants the kingdoms of this world to become the Kingdoms of our God and His Christ (Rev. 11:15).

Vision Busters

On December 17, 1995, Benny Hinn made an announcement about taking back the air waves for the Lord. His statement was intended not only for his church and ministry but for the Body of Christ in general. It reflected the fact that God is currently expanding the vision of the Church to minister to not just hundreds or even thousands of people in a confined area, but to tens of thousands and millions of people throughout the nations of the world. But we will never do it sitting around together, week after week, playing Scrabble after service. We won't do it by selling hot dogs or chocolates. God wants us to enlarge the place of our tents—to think bigger thoughts and then be prepared to act on our vision. But in order to do so, we must be willing to make the necessary changes in our thinking and practice. We must resist anything that will work to destroy or limit our vision and produce "small" thinking in relation to our goals or to God Himself. Let's examine some of these areas in detail.

1) Limited Leadership

As leaders, we must be prepared to initiate into new arenas and territories. We must do the seemingly impossible, because the Church will never do what it perceives as impossible until the leadership act first. Why? Because the Church always follow the standards of its leaders. If the leadership of a church has a benevolent, giving heart, the congregation will, invariably, have a benevolent, giving heart. A visionary leadership will produce a far-sighted, prophetic congregation. A caring or cranky leadership produces a caring or cranky church, respectively.

As leaders, we must know where we are going and then inspire others to follow us. There is a saying that goes, "If you don't know where you are going, any road will take you there." But if you don't know where you are going, how will you ever arrive? Consequently, we must be diligent to make plans and set goals.

A goal is a statement of purpose—an objective to be obtained at a future time. God intends for us to have goals. A wise man will count the cost before he embarks on a building project (Luke 14:28). Leaders must also have the understanding that even though Paul plants and Apollo waters, it is God who gives the increase (1 Cor. 3:6). In other words, we must know that it is God who will enable us to achieve our plans and goals, if we are careful to listen to His voice.

At the same time, God Himself has plans for us. Psalm 33: 10-11 tells us that the plans and purposes of God will stand throughout all generations. Even at the most difficult times in our lives, His purpose for us cannot be shaken. Jeremiah 29:11 says,

> *For I know the thoughts that I think toward you, saith the LORD, thoughts of peace, and not of evil, to give you an expected end.*

The thoughts and plans God has for us are good, and He promises to give us an expected end or outcome.

The devil would like to keep Christians quiet and subdued. He wants the Church to be like a fish in a bowl.

He wants to limit the scope of our vision so that he can limit our expansion and growth. He does not want us to reach out to the lost generations around us.

A survey was conducted in North America not too long ago which revealed that 87 percent of business company employees had no goals or vision. Should it surprise us that we continue to see so many companies declare bankruptcy? A fish, you see, will never grow beyond the size of the bowl you place it in. Neither can a business or individual expand beyond the scope of their vision. In order to fulfill what God has for us, therefore, we must look up toward our Lord and Saviour and banish all self-limitations. We have to know our identity in Christ and what He has ordained for us to accomplish.

In the same survey mentioned above, it was discovered that 10 percent of the people had general, but unwritten, goals. Only 3 percent had written goals. In the church world today, those who are on the cutting-edge of God's power are those who have goals and purposes that are written down. Whenever a ministry starts within our church, I always ask our leaders for written goals. Whether it is our youth, nursery or ushers ministries, we expect written plans detailing future accomplishments. That is the only way things will get done. If it is a written plan, you can see it. Others can see it, too. Then everyone can determine whether or not we are achieving what we set out to do.

2) Trusting in Men For Provision

The second thing that can limit vision and curb expansion is trusting in men rather than God to supply us with what we need. It is certainly true that God works through men, but our focus should be on Him alone as Provider.

I once said that I was believing God for twelve millionaires in my church. Some people were angered by my statement and felt I was going too far. Several families actually left our church because of this single incident. Was their response justified?

The truth is, the Church needs people who have the financial means and willingness to help publish the Gospel—individuals who are so completely sold out to God that every other thing (including money) is secondary. The Gospel of Luke tells us that Jesus had some very wealthy people who supported His ministry:

> *And it came to pass afterward, that he went throughout every city and village, preaching and shewing the glad tidings of the kingdom of God: and the twelve were with him, And certain women, which had been healed of evil spirits, Mary called Magdalene, out of whom went seven devils, And Joanna the wife of Chuza Herod's steward, and Susanna, and many others, which ministered unto him of their substance* (Luke 8:1-3).

You see, money itself—as a means of exchange—is not an evil thing. No, rather it is the *love* of money which is the root of many evils (1 Tim. 6:10). Consequently, it is *who has* the money that is important. Money in the hands of a covetous Christian is about the worst thing possible. But money in the hands of a sold-out believer can be a great blessing to the Kingdom of God. But trusting and putting confidence in *people* (rather than God) to supply our needs will hinder our vision and limit our ability to expand.

Unlike man's, God's resources are boundless, and He alone has the ability to ensure our heavenly vision will be fulfilled: *"Commit thy way unto the Lord; trust also in him; and he shall bring it to pass"* (Ps. 37:5).

3) Failure to Take Risks

Failing to take risks is the third way we can limit expansion in our life. Many times, when we try to do something new, our head tells us, "You can't do that!" Still, God is saying, "Do it!" Perhaps nobody has ever done what you intend to do. That doesn't mean you can't do it! It only means you will have to trust God for the results. Other people may even tell you that you cannot do what God has spoken to your heart, but don't believe them. If God has birthed it in you, it is a sure thing—if only you are willing to follow.

To risk something means to expose it to hazards or danger. Consequently, risk implies the possibility of loss or injury—something many people fear. But the Bible says that we are not to be bound by fear (Rom. 8:15). Don't sit around spinning your wheels. Nothing will happen if you do nothing. When God says, "Jump!" we need to jump. When He says "Shout!" just shout—don't let fearful thoughts deter you. God needs you to be bold and radical. He needs you to step out boldly in faith and get the job done. If we are afraid to take risks, then we are bound by fear and not living by faith. God wants us to live by faith (Hab. 2:4).

Like Peter, let us step out of the boat. Peter acted on the Word of Jesus when the Master said, "Come" and walked on water. But when he started watching the wind instead of his Master's face, he began to sink. The lesson to be learned here is that *once God tells you something and you start doing it, refuse to listen to anything contrary to that.* Just obey the prophetic word. If you listen to other voices you will fail, like King Saul (see 1 Sam. 15:24-26). Don't be concerned about pleasing people if you know you are pleasing God. It is God alone who matters in the long run.

4) Past Failures

The fourth way to hinder expansion is to allow yourself to be limited by your own past failures. The truth is, people don't always get things right the first or second time. Perhaps not even the third or fourth time. In fact, there are things I've been doing for years that I still don't do properly even now. But I haven't given up. I keep trying to do better the next time.

Henry Ford once told his engineers to build a certain kind of engine and they replied that it couldn't be done. Undaunted, he instructed them to keep working until they found a way. The project took several years and cost a great deal of money, but at the end of it came the V8 engine.

Several years ago, I saw the movie *Apollo 13*. Although I didn't like the attitude of the Mission Control Commander, he had a determined personality and a good spirit. He adamantly refused to accept each seeming impossibility and pushed his team of scientists and engineers to do things they had never done before. The lives of three astronauts were saved as a result.

One problem we have in the Church today is a "loser" mentality among many believers. Because of their past failures, they don't believe they will ever succeed. But the Bible says that we are more than conquerors through

Christ (Rom. 8:37). Jesus is the winner of all winners. He never lost a match—and we are members of Him! Make up your mind to learn from your past mistakes. Learn from your failures. Focus on the finish line and run until you win. The enemy may knock us down, but we will bounce back up again (Prov. 24:16). And when the devil sees that you keep bouncing back, he will become wary of you. So if things don't go the way you expect them to go, don't quit. Keep moving forward. Don't allow your past to determine your future.

5) Complacency

Another enemy of expansion is complacency. I like to call it "Comfort-zone Christianity." Pew-sitters, you see, abound in the Church. Many are tithers but not "divers." In other words, they don't want to be committed beyond giving money to the church. They are just too comfortable maintaining the status quo. Such people fail to recognize that even the most comfortable chair becomes uncomfortable after a while, that the most comfortable bed does not necessarily give you the rest you need. Ultimately, complacency breeds discontent, and discontent breeds criticism. It should come as no surprise then, that complacent people are often the most critical of others.

God doesn't want us to be comfortable; He wants us to be committed. He wants us to have the determined attitude that *no matter what happens, we are moving on.* Jesus wants us to "occupy" until He comes (Rev. 2:25). That means to be busy fulfilling the will of God for our lives.

"But I don't have a gift," you may say. Do you need a special gift to clean bathrooms or mop floors? "But I'm not called to do that." Well, I did both. Before I entered full-time ministry, I was faithful to have the shiniest toilets and the cleanest floors and today I have a staff of seventy and a spotless church facility! Many people are waiting for God to send them somewhere with a prophetic word. While that may happen, it is not usually the case. You must be willing to serve where you presently are, today. Dust a desk. Vacuum a carpet. Put a paintbrush to the wall. Don't be content to just sit in church. God wants you to be on your feet. Lift up the hands that hang down (Heb. 12:12).

It is such a pity that in the Church world only 10 percent of the people do 80 percent of the work. One hundred percent of the work should be done by 100 percent of the people. We should serve one another as Jesus Christ taught us by example (John 13:5).

We are not called to just give our tithes and offerings or to be pumped-up on the Word, but to be servants and witnesses of the grace of God. You may not be able to go to church more than once a week, but there are still many things you can do. Have you considered visiting a nursing home? You can give comfort to someone. How about the hospitals and prisons?

We have a volunteer couple in our church who visit more than forty nursing homes every month, who do what they do with all their hearts, as unto the Lord (Col. 3:23). Sometimes they ask for people who can play the piano and guitar or other musical instruments, other people who could minister along with them. Yet many times there are no volunteers. Perhaps those people fail to understand that when they sow love, care and affection into the elderly, they will reap those same things when they are older. It's a principle of the Word.

I can recall when I started ministering to the youth at a church in Detroit. One day there was a terrible snow storm and only one youth showed up for the meeting. But thank God for that one kid. I preached to him as if the whole room was filled! I believe God honoured that. The last I heard, that man went on to serve as a chaplain in the military.

Complacency is a spirit that comes on Christians just to keep them in the mundane, peripheral things of life. It is the Laodicean spirit of Revelation (Rev. 3:15) which results in "Sunday Morning Christianity": the practice of attending church once a week while maintaining a lifestyle that fails to reflect a living relationship with Jesus.

It is time to rise up and shine for our Lord. The fire of His Spirit burns within us, so let's fan into flame the embers in our souls. Let us be so hot for Him that those who come in contact with us can feel the heat and be drawn to its Source.

6) Traditions of Men

Traditions can be good, bad or irrelevant. But traditions of men that undermine the Word of God will hinder believers. "But that's the way Grandma used to do it," we hear. Thank God for grandparents. "We like *Amazing Grace*." Thank God for *Amazing Grace*. But let's make sure that the traditions we uphold, in turn, uphold the Word of God.

"Everybody is welcome at our church." Yes, they should be—if they are sinners in need of salvation. But not everybody is welcome at our church. The Bible says that we are not to associate with people who claim to be Christians, yet are walking in fornication, adultery, idolatry or alcoholism (1 Cor. 5:11). Why? Because their lifestyle could be transferred to others: *"A little leaven leaveneth the whole lump"* (1 Cor. 5:6). We are not to share in other people's sins. A church's leadership will give account before God concerning what happens in their congregation. Consequently, they need to be very perceptive and wise.

Traditions of men make the Word of God powerless (Mark 7:13). Someone comes up with a new idea and the traditionalists respond: "Now see here, we don't want anyone rocking this boat." They are so set in their ways that they fail to realize that Jehovah is the God of the living, not of the dead (Mark 12:27). They can't imagine God doing something they don't already know about, so they erupt in division, strife and envying.

"This is the way we used to do it at my church," some people will say. Well, if God really wanted them to leave that church, they will have to adjust to the flow of things in their new church. Otherwise, they should go back where they came from!

"But I like the way things used to be." Well, I like the way some things were, too, but if I stayed the way I used to be, I would cease to be a blessing to God and His Kingdom.

7) Going With the Crowd

Another vision robber is that age-old tendency to "go with the crowd." Crowd mentality is herd mentality. "Everyone else is doing it this way." That may be. "It's popular. It makes good sense." Perhaps, but to who?

"Shorten your service and keep it under an hour and we will pack out this place. Tune down the praise and worship. Just sing a couple of songs. Don't preach about tithes and offerings because people will just think you want their money. Don't preach about holiness or commitment. We will love everybody and they will love us." Suggestions like these may make sense to our minds, but their source is not God.

People don't need to like us. They didn't all like Jesus. If everybody loves us, we are probably backslidden! If everybody speaks kindly of us, we are probably compromising the gospel. God doesn't need anybody's vote. He's already elected Jesus as our Lord and appointed Him to die in our place so that we can live for Him. We should be very careful about who we try to please.

We must always put things in proper perspective. The book of James tells us that friendship with the world is the same as enmity with God (Jas. 4:4). The majority may always carry the vote, but the One who lives in you is greater than the greatest majority.

8) Selfishness

Great goals are never achieved by an individual acting alone. Great goals are only achieved by individuals functioning as a team. Selfishness, therefore, is an enemy of expansion. Insomuch as there are some "big" names in the Bible, there are also a host of "little" names—helpers or associates—who helped those men accomplish God's purpose for them. God's intention isn't to enlist a bunch of lone rangers who will take all the credit for themselves. No, He is interested in teamwork.

Thank God for those who held Moses' hands while Israel fought the Amalekites (Exod. 17:12). Thank God for

Caleb and Joshua. Thank God for Noah's sons and their wives. And thank God for all the supporters of Paul's ministry, from Ananias and Barnabas to Timothy and Titus.

Selfish people lack a team spirit. The members of Christ's Body need one another. Whether you like it or not, I need you and you need me. Some people say, "Oh, I just need Jesus." Yes, you need Jesus, but you don't need *just* Jesus. As members of God's family, we depend on each other. 1 Corinthians 12:24-25 reads:

> *For our comely parts have no need: but God hath tempered the body together, having given more abundant honour to that part which lacked: That there should be no schism in the body; but that the members should have the same care one for another.*

The sooner we recognize that we are a team—without competition and haughtiness—the easier it will be for us to advance the Kingdom of our Lord in this world.

THREE

Stretch Forth

"...let them stretch forth the curtains of thine habitations..." (Isa. 54:2).

The second law of expansion is to "stretch forth." To stretch forth means to spread out or to exercise something beyond normal limits. It implies elasticity. And for the purpose of our study, we could say it also means *going one step farther*.

There are many areas of our life that God wants us to "stretch forth" in, but before we explore these in detail, I would first like to make some general statements about what God has already invested in you.

The "Putting" Business

The Word teaches us that God has given you everything you need to lead a life that is well-pleasing to Him (2 Pet. 1:3). In other words, there is nothing you need that God hasn't already put inside of you. As the following Scriptures indicate, God is in the "putting" business.

Thou hast put gladness in my heart … (Ps. 4:7).

And I will give them one heart, and I will put a new spirit within you … (Ezek.11:19).

I will put my laws in their inward parts, and write it in their hearts … (Jer. 31:33).

Who hath put wisdom in the inward parts? or who hath given understanding to the heart? (Job 38:36).

Gladness, a new spirit, His law, wisdom and understanding—God has put these and many other things inside each of us for His own purposes. And he expects a return for everything He has invested in us (Matt. 25:27).

Afraid to Stretch

Many people won't allow themselves to be stretched because of fear—fear of failure, fear of men, fear of the unknown, fear of embarrassment, rejection or isolation. Any of these fears can prevent you from stretching. Closely related to fear is doubt. You may want to step out, but you're just not sure. Inside you're asking yourself, "What if?" What if something goes wrong? What if it doesn't work? If you miss the mark, just praise God and try again until it works. It is a well-known fact that quitters never win. Winners never quit, either. *"Be of good cheer,"* Jesus said, *"I have overcome the world"* (John 16:33). Never forget that the Spirit of a Champion lives in you—and He never loses!

Don't be afraid to stretch. If you are following God's plan, He will support you. If you stretch forth your hand in faith, He will stretch forth His.

Procrastination

I own an expensive exercise machine. It could be sitting in my office or at home and I could look at it and say, "Tomorrow is the first day of the year. I will start exercising tomorrow." The world is full of people who say, "Tomorrow I'm going to do it." And tomorrow came and went, just like yesterday, and they never did what they had planned to do.

"Tomorrow I'm going to quit smoking." Why tomorrow? Why not today? The day of determination shouldn't be postponed. Faith is always in the present tense. Hebrews 11:1 says, *"Now faith is..."* Faith is putting action to your belief—today. If I don't get on my exercise machine today, I'll probably not get on it tomorrow. A wise man once said, "Don't postpone until tomorrow what you can do today." Tomorrow will always come and go.

Other people say, "I will get around to it." But many of them never "get around to it." Acts 17:32-34 contains a marvelous illustration relating to our discussion. It shows three distinct responses to the resurrection, which we could apply to any area of stretching. The irreverent Greeks mocked the resurrection. The procrastinators said, "We will hear thee again." But those who were interested in the message made a decisive move. Right then and there, they joined themselves to Paul and became believers.

Procrastination will prevent you from stretching to enter new arenas in your walk with God. Procrastinators never enter into God's abundant life. Matthew 8:21-22 depicts a procrastinating disciple:

And another of his disciples said unto him, Lord, suffer me first to go and bury my father. But Jesus said unto him, Follow me, and let the dead bury their dead.

History tells us that Jewish custom dictated that the body had to be buried by sunrise of the following day. In all likelihood, however, the man's father wasn't even dead yet. And Jesus' response? Follow me—right now, right here, today. Another similar account is contained in Luke 9:61-62:

And another also said, Lord I will follow thee; but let me first go bid them farewell, which are at home at my house. And Jesus said unto him, No man, having put his hand to the plough, and looking back, is fit for the kingdom of God.

This young man wanted to go and say goodbye to his family. But judging by the Jesus' response, it seems safe to conclude that this man had already had time to count the cost. It is very possible that if he went back home he would have been talked right out of doing God's will for his life.

Many people have been talked out of doing God's will. I was amazed many years ago when I made the decision to attend Bible school that many of my closest friends (who earlier encouraged me in the faith) spoke against it. They thought I was crazy to think of leaving my job. "How are you going to provide for your family?" some of them asked. Their concerns were thoughtful perhaps, but I had clear direction from God. He said, "Go," and I was determined to obey. In the final analysis, He didn't let me down in any way. In fact, after graduation, I returned home from Bible school with many testimonies of God's faithfulness to me during that time.

Discipline is Needed

Stretching, or growth, is only possible if we are willing to pay the price. The price we pay is *discipline*. The words discipline and disciple are closely related. Literally, a disciple is a disciplined follower of Jesus Christ.

Discipline doesn't come overnight. It takes time to develop. As mentioned earlier, to stretch something means to exercise it beyond its normal or ordinary limits. Consequently, stretching usually implies discomfort. Stretching breaks our long-established comfort zones and shatters complacency. Discipline is essentially *the ability to keep at something despite one's feelings to the contrary.* A disciplined person has a goal and painstakingly applies himself to that goal, refusing to find an easy way out. It should go without saying that a disciplined person does not procrastinate; discipline requires decisiveness and action.

Most of us have patterns of procrastination or a lack of discipline in some area of our life. Most of us have also resolved, at one time or another, to improve in these areas and have failed. How can we go about breaking these long-established patterns? What follows are some practical ways we can eliminate procrastination from our lives and learn to exercise a greater level of discipline so that we can decisively respond when God gives us the opportunity to stretch.

1) Starting Small

A very simple mistake we often make when we try to do something new or different is to bite off more than we can chew. Practically speaking, you probably won't experience success if you start off with unrealistically high goals. Don't attempt to pray for an hour every day, for example, when you haven't yet tried praying for five minutes. You might find yourself looking at the clock every minute. And that is not what the Bible means by watching and praying! If you haven't read your Bible before, don't attempt to ready twenty chapters a day. You can't do it. You will find it to be a very intimidating task, and not only that, you probably won't remember anything you read! Besides, the Bible was not intended to be a burden to you, but something enjoyable and full of inspiration for your life.

Instead, read one chapter each day, and as you understand that and meditate on it, you can read more. That is when the Word of God blesses you. Some people attempt to read the whole Bible in a year and they can't live up to their commitment. Sometimes this brings them under condemnation. But remember, child of God, it is not how much you read, but how much illumination you have and how you let the light of God direct your life that makes the difference.

Start small. Don't set unrealistic goals for yourself. That will frustrate you. Maybe you work ten hours a day, six days a week. Then you come home to your children who need time with you. Yet you think you can spend an hour each in the Word and in prayer. You're setting yourself up for frustration. Who requires that from you? God would rather you spend fifteen minutes of enjoyable time with Him than two hours of frustration. Don't you think God knows you're raising children?

Many Christians backslide because someone puts the letter of the law (instead of the law of the Spirit) on them.

They walk around full of condemnation, thinking they've failed God because they didn't measure up to someone else's standard. How will they be able to pray the effectual prayer of a righteous man (Jas. 5:16) when they feel anything but righteous? Many people are robbed of God's blessings in this way.

Now let's return to our exercise machine illustration for a moment. If I haven't used that machine for a while it would be foolish of me to spend a whole hour on it today, wouldn't it? Why? Because by tomorrow I would be in bad shape. The muscles that hadn't been used would have been unwisely and suddenly stretched, resulting in aches and pains. The best thing for me to do would be to start small. Maybe I can spend five minutes today, ten minutes tomorrow and fifteen minutes the day after. I can progressively increase the time as I get used to the exercise regimen. Only then can I reap the full benefits of bodily exercise.

What would happen if I just decided to go a full hour on the exerciser anyway? Things might be fine for the first five minutes. But after ten minutes things would be getting harder. After twenty minutes I'd be puffing and wheezing. In half an hour I might be ready to die! My muscles haven't been stretched enough to go the long haul. When we allow ourselves to be stretched in any way, we need to be careful about moving too quickly. You don't want the elastic to snap!

If your muscles of faith and love, your muscles of self-control and goodness, your muscles of prayer and worship have never been stretched, it won't be easy for you to go the long haul. So do it gradually. Avoid setting unrealistic goals or you're sure to fall short of your own expectations. You may start off with great momentum, but it's enduring to the end—how you finish—that matters most (see Rev. 2:5).

God wants us to do spiritual exercises, but He starts us off slowly. That's why He first feeds us with the milk of His Word before the meat (1 Cor. 3:2; Heb 5:12-14; 1 Pet. 2:2). He won't give us a diet that won't be beneficial to us. He first meets us where we are, and then gradually brings us to where He wants us to be.

Nobody starts at the finish line. In our walk of faith and love, and in our acts of goodness and self-control, we graduate from one level to another. God translates us from glory to glory (2 Cor. 3:18). So let us take things gradually at first and increase the pace in time. Remember, God reveals Himself to those who first *diligently* and *consistently* seek Him (see Jer. 29:13).

2) Focusing

Often, people get sidetracked because they try to do too many things at once. Even in the local church, an individual can be so busy running around in different directions that they never get anything done. It would be better to focus on one task and complete it, than to perpetually struggle with multiple tasks. It is better to do one thing right than a dozen things wrong.

Many people in the Church are robbed of the joy of the Lord for this very reason. Some who were divinely ordained to be in the music ministry get involved in other ministries. Others who love children and are ordained to be in the nursery spend their time in other areas—usually because someone else got them involved. Don't let other people drag you into a ministry you can't whole-heartedly and joyfully function in. We all need to be labouring in an area where God can cause us to flourish. God has enough people in the Church who are called to meet the needs in the various areas. We should know His calling on our lives and stick to it.

If you have the anointing to be a counsellor, don't involve yourself in two or five other areas; that will breed frustration. If you are called to be an usher, be the best usher in the church. Be what you are called to be and you will enjoy God in the process.

"If I don't do this, nobody else will do it," you may say. Maybe that's why you're frustrated. God may already have someone waiting in the wings who is presently being hindered by your frantic activities. So get out of the way!

"But I don't want to let it go," you respond. Of course, that is the real problem. You want to run the show, but the show is not yours to run! It's time you learned how to get out of the way and allow God to manifest His power in the way—and through whom—He desires.

Whatever I do today is done with joy. Over the years, I stopped doing a lot of things that used to frustrate me, and God raised up faithful men and women to take care of the many areas of ministry I used to worry about. I don't try to function in ten different areas any more. As Senior Pastor, I am now free to devote myself to my primary function—prayer and the ministry of the Word. I minister in one major area: feeding the flock of God. And I am very happy working in the place God has ordained for me.

Besides being able to serve God with joy, the Bible also teaches that the Word and the knowledge of God increases when people focus on their gifts and calling. The account of Acts 6:1-7 beautifully illustrates this fact:

And in those days, when the number of the disciples was multiplied, there arose a murmuring of the Grecians against the Hebrews, because their widows were neglected in the daily ministration. Then the twelve called the multitude of the disciples unto them, and said, It is not reason that we should leave the word of God, and serve tables. Wherefore, brethren, look ye out among you seven men of honest report, full of the Holy Ghost and wisdom, whom we may appoint over this business. But we will give ourselves continually to prayer, and to the ministry of the word. And the saying pleased the whole multitude: and they chose Stephen, a man full of faith and of the Holy Ghost, and Philip, and Prochorus, and Nicanor, and Timon, and Parmenas, and Nicolas a proselyte of Antioch: Whom they set before the apostles: and when they had prayed, they laid their hands on them. And the word of God increased; and the number of the disciples multiplied in Jerusalem greatly; and a great company of the priests were obedient to the faith.

If you decide to focus on God's personal calling for your life, both you and God's Kingdom will benefit.

As we learn to focus on one area of ministry in order to minimize or eliminate frustration, we can also tackle one area of our habits in order to aid our growth in God. What is the most frustrating issue in your life today? What is your worst habit? Let that be the first thing you attack for the next two months. Fight it, resist it, and in time you'll break it, guaranteed—if you work on it with God's strength.

Don't try to attack five different problem areas or habits at the same time. You will become overwhelmed and frustrated. Instead, choose a habit and work on it today, tomorrow, next week, next month—until you break its hold on you. Because habits are formed over a period of time (sometimes many years), is it reasonable to expect to conquer in one week what you spent the last twenty years acquiring? You can't break a thirty-year old habit in three days! It takes time and discipline.

Of course, not all habits are bad. Although habits generally connote something negative in our culture today, there are also good, positive habits. Scripture tells us that Jesus had the habit of praying very early in the morning (Mark 1:35). That was a good habit. But remember, every habit is a *learned behaviour*. Good habits as well as bad habits are formed over a period of time. We may do things initially, without much planning, but as we consistently do them, they become habits in our lives.

Many people smoke today, not because they are bound by nicotine, but because it is a habit. Other people habitually indulge in food because that's all they know how to do! Good habits are developed the same way. As we persevere in something we desire to be a part of our lives, like arriving at church early or putting others first, it will eventually become a habit that pleases God and is a blessing to us. The problem is that many people don't want to devote a day, a week, two months or a whole year on one problem or issue. Consequently, they never stretch in the things of God the way they would like.

Consistency is the key—and there will be no consistency without focus. Focus your time and energy on the area God has called you to. Eliminate your bad habits one by one. Develop new habits as the Spirit leads. Maintaining your focus will help you to eliminate procrastination and develop a disciplined life. If you do, you will find yourself more rapidly progressing in the things of God.

3) Organizing

Another way to help combat procrastination and poor discipline is to organize. Organizing is not so much a spiritual issue as it is a common sense one. Disorganized people—whether they are Christians or not—almost never reach their goals. They lack purpose and vision. If you're disorganized, it is easy enough to become organized if you're determined to make the necessary changes. You can start simply by writing things down. It helps you to remember what you intend to do later.

As a pastor, Sunday is my busiest day. By the end of the day I have pockets full of notes, which might include telephone numbers, reminders, prayer requests and so on. I don't think I would ever remember any of those things if I didn't write them down. So instead of trying to remember everything that happened at the end of each day, I just pull out my notes and go through them, one by one. This makes for a more efficient use of time in the long run. It also makes me more effective in service because it helps to ensure that I get everything done.

Can you imagine what would happen if someone asked me after service to remember her Aunt Lily in my prayers, and I didn't write it down? You see, on Sundays I'm trying to greet hundreds of people as well as remember their names, shake their hands, and engage in a bit of conversation. Without writing things down I would be doomed. After the hustle and bustle of a busy day, a prayer request would be quickly forgotten. Consequently, I usually ask people to write things down for me. Or I might just agree in prayer with them on the spot if there aren't too many people waiting to talk to me.

Organization is essential. I'm not implying that we tune out the Holy Spirit, but that we give Him avenues to work in. Before Jesus Christ multiplied the bread and fish, He organized the people into groups (Mark 6:39-40). The miracles occurred after the people were organized.

The first aspect of organization for you could be to have a *written list*. Use a day-planner if you have one. My wife sometimes has a list of twenty things she wants to accomplish in a day. She checks them off one by one as she completes each task. At the end of the day she can then determine how productive her day has been.

The second would be to *prioritize your list*. Assign the tasks values of importance. Start from the most important to the least. As the day progresses, you will realize that the important things have been achieved. The less important things can be done if there's enough time left.

Third, *organize your day at the best time*. Each of us is different. Some function best at night, others during the early hours of the day. You should determine when is best for you and work accordingly.

Fourth, *use a calendar*. Don't plan so much in a week that you can't keep up. It's true we've been talking about stretching, but you must also be realistic, too. Don't bite off more than you can chew. Burning out is not the same as stretching.

Fifth, *be accountable to someone.* Answer to someone—your wife, husband, children or a friend—for what you are getting done.

Now that we have addressed some of the things that could hinder our ability to be stretched by God, let's examine some of the areas God wants us to be stretched in.

Stretching Areas

One of the most important areas God wants us to be stretched in, is in the area of faith. We must understand that when we stretch our faith we enter into the realm of the miraculous. All the way through the Word of God, whenever there is a *stretching forth,* there is a manifestation of the miraculous. In Exodus, Moses *stretched forth* his hand and divided the Red Sea (Exod. 14:21). He stretched it again to drown the armies of Egypt (Exod. 14:27). Joshua *stretched forth* his hand toward the city of Ai and God gave it into his hands (Josh. 8:18). David *stretched forth* his hands to God and was delivered (Ps. 143:6). In each instance, there was a stretching forth of a hand. But whose hand was actually getting the job done? God's, of course—not man's. The early Church, too, recognized that while they did many wonderful miracles, it was *God's* hand, not theirs, that was really at work:

And now, Lord, behold their threatenings: and grant unto thy servants, that with all boldness they may speak thy word, By stretching forth thine hand to heal; and

*that signs and wonders may be done by the name of thy
holy child Jesus (Acts 4:29-30).*

The principle is simply this: as we stretch forth our
hands in faith, God's hand moves in response, bringing His
power and presence into people's hearts and lives. Demon
bondages are broken by it and the captives are delivered.

God wants us to be stretched in the miraculous. Every
great person in history and every inventor was stretched in
the course of their quest. Many of them failed many, many
times before finally reaching the mark. You see, God has
put His creativity inside us, but that creativity needs to be
challenged to produce for His glory.

God also wants us to be stretched in His Word. 2 Peter
3:18 says, *"But grow in grace, and in the knowledge of our Lord
and Saviour Jesus Christ."* How does one grow in the
knowledge of God? Through the Word, of course. The
Word shows us who God is. Once we possess the knowledge of God, we are able to act in faith on the basis of that
knowledge and do the seemingly impossible. All things
are possible to those who believe God's Word (Mark 9:23).
If you believe something is impossible, your vision will be
limited. But we serve the God of the impossible. Remember that He can do all things in and through us because
His Word says so!

From a natural standpoint, it was impossible for the Red
Sea to split and for millions of people to walk through it on
dry ground. It was impossible for hungry lions to shut their
mouths when a prey was thrown into their den. It was
impossible for the furnace fire not to burn the three Hebrew
children. But when the individuals steeped in these crises

stepped out of the realm of the possible, the God of the impossible stepped in to save them. Glory to God!

Remember the man with the withered hand? Jesus told him, *"Stretch forth thine hand"* (Mark 3:5), and even though the man didn't have a proper hand, as he exercised whatever muscles remained of it, his hand was fully restored. Note that the miracle came when he *stretched*. The miracle will come for you and for me when we stretch, as well.

God also wants us stretched in faith and in love. When you meet people who are unlovable, your love muscles will be stretched. Allow God to perfect His love in and through you.

Your patience will be stretched by the circumstances that come against you. God expects you to stand and to maintain a good confession.

Your ability to give will also be stretched. But the Bible promises that when you give, it will be given back to you (Luke 6:38). And as you give, mix your giving with gladness, recognizing that God is ultimately the owner of everything.

You will be also stretched in your witnessing. It doesn't matter if you don't know many Scriptures. Let your life speak out loudly. Let your love be experienced by others. Be sensitive to the Holy Spirit so you will know what to say, when to say it and to whom.

Above all, you will be stretched in the miraculous as God reveals Himself to you. Deuteronomy 4:34; 5:15 and 7:19 all show how God's outstretched arm wrought miracles for His people, the Israelites. If He did it then, He will do it now. Allow God to use you as an instrument to display his miraculous power to the world. Be willing to stretch and be stretched.

FOUR

Spare Not

"...spare not..." (Isa. 54:2).

W e have already been instructed to "enlarge" and to "stretch out." The third law of expansion is "spare not," which means *don't hold back!* Don't refuse, restrain or hold anything back from God. The command to "spare not" is actually a command to break the covetous spirit of the world and give your all to God.

What Are You Holding Back?

Is there anything you're holding back from God today? Do you have talents that God wants to tap into? Or are you too busy to have time for the things of God? Take the time today to reschedule your programs and readjust your priorities. Let the things of God be your first consideration.

Perhaps you already know what your talents are, but you're not sure God wants to use them in the Church. Well, He does! You were created for His pleasure and anything He gives to you really belongs to Him. So why hold back? Is it because your church leadership can't accept your giftings? That could actually be a sign for you to utilize your talents in the secular market to the glory of God!

God has been speaking to a lot of Christians about this very thing over the years. But perhaps because they can't expand their thinking, they haven't responded. Maybe they feel inadequate or even unbelieving. Or could it be that what they have in mind has never been seen or done before? Are any of these good reasons to withdraw in fear from the will of the Almighty?

Has God blown your mind with vivid imaginations? Do you think your vision is unattainable? Don't withhold yourself from Him. Allow yourself to dream a bit. God will bring supernatural resources to you for the fulfillment of His purposes in your life. His resources are beyond your imagination:

Now unto him that is able to do exceeding abundantly above all that we ask or think, according to the power that worketh in us (Eph. 3:20).

That is a biblical fact!

Don't hold back your talents, gifts or resources from God. Put your hand to the plough and start serving Him today. It doesn't matter how long you've been resisting His leading. Today is a new day. Use it to do something for the King of kings. Use your time for God and not just for television. Use your energy for God, not just for sports. Use your finances for God, not just for pleasure. There is nothing wrong with television, sports or pleasure. But we err when we value these things more highly than we value God.

"But I don't have time to get involved in the church," you say. That's fine, as long as it is not a lie. But if you have time to watch the television for two hours a day, but not enough time to help out at your church, something is wrong. The message you are sending to the cloud of heavenly witnesses is that your TV time is more important than Kingdom time. Use your time and talents for God and not just for a pay cheque. Use your expertise for God. Get committed and involved in the church.

Let's look at a passage of Scripture related to our current discussion:

> *The desire of the righteous is only good: but the expectation of the wicked is wrath. There is that scattereth, and yet increaseth; and there is that withholdeth more than is meet, but it tendeth to poverty. The liberal soul shall be made fat: and he that watereth shall be watered also himself. He that withholdeth corn, the people shall curse him: but blessing shall be upon the head of him that selleth it* (Prov. 11:23-26).

Notice what this passage says about the person who "withholdeth more than is meet." It says that he "tendeth to poverty." Although this principle is discussed in the context of finances, it applies to other areas of our lives where we are "withholding" things from God's service.

Whatever skills you have can be used for Him. Remember the parable of the talents? If you don't use what God gives you, He might take it back and give it to someone who will (see Matt. 25:14-30).

Maybe you think that what God's given you doesn't amount to much. But have you used what you've been given? Or are you too busy comparing your gifts with someone else's to put them into service—like the fellow with the single talent who hid his Lord's money in the ground (Matt. 25:18)? And what was the result?

Then he which had received the one talent came and said, Lord, I knew thee that thou art an hard man, reaping where thou hast not sown, and gathering where thou hast not strawed: And I was afraid, and went and hid thy talent in the earth: lo, there thou hast that is thine. His lord answered and said unto him, Thou wicked and slothful servant, thou knewest that I reap where I sowed not, and gather where I have not strawed: Thou oughtest therefore to have put my money to the exchangers, and then at my coming I should have received mine own with usury. Take therefore the talent from him, and give it unto him which hath ten talents (Matt. 25:24-28).

The story indicates that the least the man should have done was to invest the talent in order to earn interest on it. Then there would have been a tangible gain for both himself and the Master.

If God gives you a little, use the little. If He gives you much, use much. He wants you to give proportionally to what you have: *"For unto whomsoever much is given, of him shall be much required"* (Luke 12:48). God wouldn't ask you for what you don't have. But neither will He tolerate your withholding from Him what you do have.

You may not fully recognize today the vastness and depth of what He has invested in you. If not, simply continue to walk with Him in the light you have and dedicate your entire being to Him. Your willingness to obey Him in everything puts you in a vantage point of success in life and will enable God to reveal Himself more fully in you.

Use what God has given you or lose it. God has given some people heavenly languages they haven't used for years! And they wonder why they are so unfulfilled. A clear command is given in Jude 20: *"But ye, beloved, building up yourselves on your most holy faith, praying in the Holy Ghost."* If you don't build yourself up, you will be weak. Is it any wonder so many Christians are weak?

Don't withhold anything from God. Don't relent in your pursuit of heavenly treasure. "Spare not," the Bible says. Don't restrain. Don't withhold.

In point of fact, it is actually not enough to merely refrain from withholding; we must be actively benevolent:

> *Withhold not good from them to whom it is due, when it is in the power of thine hand to do it. Say not unto thy neighbour, Go, and come again, and to morrow I will give; when thou hast it by thee* (Prov. 3:27-28).

> *In the morning sow thy seed, and in the evening withhold not thine hand: for thou knowest not whether shall prosper, either this or that, or whether they both shall be alike good* (Eccl. 11:6).

In other words, benevolence is not something you should stop doing. Don't take a vacation from doing good. Be consistently benevolent toward God and your neighbour.

The story of the Good Samaritan (Luke 10:30-37) provides an excellent illustration. A man had been robbed and wounded by common thieves. A priest saw him and crossed to the other side of the street. A Levite saw him and went the other way. They both withheld care and mercy. They held back kindness and grace. But a stranger saw the wounded man and rushed to lend a helping hand. He treated the unfortunate fellow like his own flesh and blood. And since he couldn't adequately offer medical help, he took the man to the hospital and paid the necessary fees. Jesus used his actions to show what true benevolence looks like.

God wants us to release the many things He's given us so that He can expand and enlarge us to accomplish His purposes. Don't belittle your God-given talents and abilities. Put them into practice. Use what you have and God will increase what you have. With Him and through Him there's nothing we can't do, so let's take off all the limitations and give him our all.

Be Totally Immersed

God wants us to be totally submerged in the river of His Spirit so that He will be able to move us wherever He wants us. He doesn't want any half measures. He wants to fill us to overflowing and transport us from glory to glory (2 Cor. 3:18). The prophet Ezekiel prophesied about this river of the Spirit:

> *Afterward he brought me again unto the door of the house; and, behold, waters issued out from under the threshold of the house eastward... And when the man that had the line in his hand went forth eastward, he measured a thousand cubits, and he brought me through the waters; the waters were to the ankles. Again he measured a thousand, and brought me through the waters; the waters were to the knees. Again he measured a thousand, and brought me through; the waters were to the loins. Afterward he measured a thousand; and it was a*

river that I could not pass over: for the waters were risen, waters to swim in, a river that could not be passed over... Then said he unto me, These waters issue out toward the east country, and go down into the desert, and go into the sea: which being brought forth into the sea, the waters shall be healed. And it shall come to pass, that every thing that liveth, which moveth, whithersoever the rivers shall come, shall live... (Ezek. 47:1-9).

Notice that at first the water was only ankle-deep. You can run quickly in water as shallow as that, though not be as swiftly as you normally would. But it's a different story when the water reaches your knees and then your waist. Movement will be impeded and you could easily fall—especially if there is a current. Nevertheless, you could still pass through it to the other side.

Soon, however, you are all the way under. The water is over your head. Now you can't cross the river unless you swim. Note that in this prophecy, life and healing came about only when there was *total immersion*. That means total submission to God and His will for our lives. Only then can His purpose be realized in spite of the adverse circumstances life brings our way.

Many songs are being sung today about jumping into the river of God. The Bible says that Jesus has caused rivers of living water to flow out of us (John 7:38). We are in the "river" time. But God doesn't want us to wade in only to our ankles, knees or waist. He wants us to be totally immersed—to the point where we die to ourselves and let the Life inside us emerge and be seen. Determine to go all the way with God. Nothing lacking. Nothing withheld. Spare not!

Romans 6:13 commands us to "yield" ourselves to God. If you see a traffic sign that says "Yield," you are supposed to pause and check for other vehicles. Any vehicle that appears has the right of way. In the same manner, we are to yield to God and let Him have the right of way.

The question all of us must soberly ask ourselves is, "Who are we supposed to live for—ourselves or the Lord?" The Word tells us that Jesus Christ has redeemed us and called us to Himself (2 Cor. 5:18). It also teaches that the proper response to this immeasurable gift is to consider ourselves dead to sin and alive to His righteousness (Rom. 6:11).

Have you been yielding to God or to your own desires? God can only increase you when you follow—or begin showing a willingness to follow—His agenda for your life. Spare not! Do not withhold anything. And yield!

FIVE

Lengthen Thy Cords

"...lengthen thy cords..." (Isa. 54:2).

After we have enlarged, stretched and spared not, God next instructs us to "lengthen thy cords." The Hebrew word translated as *lengthen* in the King James Version is elsewhere translated "draw out." The spiritual connotation is that of *reaching out to others*. You will recall that in the Great Commission, Jesus instructed us to teach the precepts of His Kingdom to all nations:

> *Go ye therefore, and teach all nations, baptizing them in the name of the Father, and of the Son, and of the Holy Ghost: Teaching them to observe all things whatsoever I have commanded you: and, lo, I am with you alway, even unto the end of the world. Amen.* (Matt. 28:19-20).

The word translated "teach" in this Scripture actually means "to disciple."[2] In other words, God wants us to make *disciples* of all nations. You see, God longs to reproduce Himself in us. That's why He invested not just talents and abilities, but His very self in us.

The Lord has always been in the business of reproduction. The book of Genesis teaches us that He commanded everything to produce after its own kind (Gen. 1:24). Jesus said that He was the Light of the world (John 8:12). But He didn't stop there. He then called on us to be lights, as well (Acts 13:47). That is reproduction in action.

Part of the process of reproducing God in us is to reproduce the works of Jesus. This means reaching out and sharing the Good News of the Gospel with others—just as Jesus did in His ministry. Making disciples, therefore, is the business of every believer. It is also a law of expansion in God's Kingdom.

God wants us to take the Good News to the people around us. He wants each of us to be an "evangelist." It is interesting that the first person to share the Good News about Christ's resurrection was neither a prophet nor a teacher. It was Mary, from whom seven demons had once been cast out (Mark 16:9). Mary had neither a religious rank nor a pulpit. But when she shared the Good News, the disciples raced each other to the site of the grave (John 20:4)!

You see, God hasn't called just the five-fold ministry gifts to evangelize. He has called all Christians to do it. In fact, the main purpose of your pastor is not really to evangelize, but to equip the ordinary folks in the church to do the work of ministry (Eph. 4:11-12). Pastors are to train their congregations to be "evangelists." Church people have the potential of being in contact with unbelievers everywhere they go—at work, at the grocery store, at the park. We should all be witnesses of Christ wherever we find ourselves.

Pastors relate to their flocks. The flocks, in turn, relate to people in all walks of life. These are the people Jesus died for. These are the people we must reach with the Good News. Pastors can't personally do very much to reach these people, no matter what church programs are in place. It is the responsibility of all Christians to reach their neighbourhoods for Christ.

People who are saved in church are usually not brought in by the pastor. Rather, church members bring their friends to service to hear the Word and experience the presence of God. That is the least a Christian should do. The ability to quote chapters and verses of Scriptures to people is not required. Simply tell them of Jesus' love and sacrifice and let the Light of God shine on them. Invite them to church. You don't need to convict or convince anyone—that's the job of the Holy Spirit.

There are places you go every day that your pastor can't step into. That's where you are supposed to be a witness. Pastors, as individuals, can still knock on doors and preach. They can share the gospel at shopping malls or on the streets, but their primary responsibility is to train the congregation to do those things. Christians are supposed to reproduce themselves everywhere they go. Paul and Silas reproduced themselves in jailers and guards (see Acts 16:27-34). Imagine how quickly the Gospel would spread if each Christian were to reach only one person each year!

A disciple is a pupil—a learner or student. You are never too old to make students for Christ. Tell them what God has done in your life and the Holy Spirit will minister to their hearts. Lengthen your cords. Let down your nets and the Lord will cause the fish to swim into them!

Making Disciples

In order to make disciples, we must first be disciples ourselves. How can you bring someone somewhere you haven't been? How can you make someone something you are not? Only disciples can disciple others. But how does one become an effective disciple—one who wholeheartedly serves God and has the ability to reproduce himself in others? Let's examine some of the principles of discipleship from the Word of God.

1) Crucifying the Flesh

We know that our spirit is regenerated at the time of our new birth in Christ (Titus 3:5). Our soul, on the other hand (i.e. our mind, emotions and intellect) must be renewed with God's Word (Rom. 12:2) so it works in co-operation with our spirit to accomplish God's will. This is because it is in our soul where we make the decisions which affect the course of our lives. However, if our soul joins forces with our *flesh* instead of our spirit, we will be continually falling into sin. That is why God's Word instructs us to "mortify"—put to death—the deeds of the flesh and follow the lead of the Spirit:

> *For if ye live after the flesh, ye shall die: but if ye through the Spirit do mortify the deeds of the body, ye shall live"* (Rom. 8:13).

The Bible teaches that crucifying the flesh and all its affections is a prerequisite for spirit life and godly rewards. Jesus said it this way:

> *If any man will come after me, let him deny himself, and take up his cross, and follow me. For whosoever will save his life shall lose it: and whosoever will lose his life for my sake shall find it* (Matt. 16:24-25).

It is human nature to crave praise and adoration. Human nature is a celebration of self. Most of the time, man wants to be comfortable. He wants to be served and catered to. He wants to be waited upon. But God wants human nature to die so that His godly nature can emerge. In other words, denying self is doing the opposite of what we "naturally" desire. It is serving instead of seeking to be served. That is the principle Jesus lived by. It is also the reason God exalted Him:

> *Let this mind be in you, which was also in Christ Jesus: Who, being in the form of God, thought it not robbery to be equal with God: But made himself of no reputation, and took upon him the form of a servant, and was made in the likeness of men: And being found in fashion as a man, he humbled himself, and became obedient unto death, even the death of the cross. Wherefore God also hath highly exalted him, and given him a name which is above every name: That at the name of Jesus every knee should bow, of things in heaven, and things in earth, and things under the earth; And that every tongue should confess that Jesus Christ is Lord, to the glory of God the Father* (Phil. 2:5-11).

Many Christians today would rather be masters than disciples. They would prefer to pick and choose where they will go and what they will hear. They go to a church where they feel comfortable and don't have to commit to anything. Many believers have itching ears and would rather not receive instruction about commitment, sacrifice or dying to self. They would rather hear about prosperity than holiness. They don't want to hear about taking up their cross, humbling themselves and serving one another. Yet these are the very things Jesus taught us through the example of His life.

The cross is a place of death. Places of death are neither fun nor interesting. But our Lord Jesus did not despise His death on the cross because He had His eyes on the glory that would follow it (Heb. 12:2). Laying our lives down on His cross is a choice we need to make. We need to die to our pride, selfish ways and interests and get on God's program. Only then will we know what life is really about.

Jesus wants you to have an abundant life (John 10:10), but many Christians don't enter into that abundant life. Why not? Because you must go to the cross before the abundant life of Christ can be manifested in you. You must die to yourself before you can lay hold of the promises of God.

I know that if Jesus were here today, He wouldn't be found hanging out in front of the television all day long. Neither would He watch some of the movies believers watch. If each of us were really to put the interests of the Kingdom first, we probably wouldn't do many of the things we are presently doing. As long as we refuse to put God's interests ahead of our own, we are doomed to stay in the outer edges of Christianity, unable to walk in the real blessings of it. And a distant walk with God won't do us any good. Peter followed Jesus "afar off" only when he was in denial (Mark 14:54).

As a pastor, I want a deeper walk with God. I want to be great in his Kingdom by being a servant. I want to build a great church for God—not in terms of numbers, but in terms of service. Moses and Joshua were servants, but we are called "sons." Becoming a servant of God is a choice we must make. It is a choice born out of our relationship with our Father: because we love God, we choose to do the right thing.

Crucify the flesh. Take up your cross and follow Him. That's what true discipleship is all about. When you selflessly lay down your life for your brother, when you invest yourself and your time into another person and you see that person grow, develop and reproduce—know that you're doing something worthwhile for God.

2) Prioritizing

The second principle of discipleship is to prioritize. How does prioritizing fit into the picture? Let's examine what Jesus had to say about priorities in Luke 14:

> *And there went great multitudes with him: and he turned, and said unto them, If any man come to me, and hate not his father, and mother, and wife, and children, and brethren, and sisters, yea, and his own life also, he cannot be my disciple* (Luke 14:25-26).

We must understand that in this context the word *hate* is indicative of priority. The implication is this: Jesus must be incomparable to our parents, spouses and families— even our own lives. Nothing and no one should be as important to us as God. No one should come before Christ in our lives and decisions.

Many Christians use excuses like, "If my spouse comes to the Lord, then I'll get involved." What you should know is that even if your spouse doesn't acknowledge the existence of God, you will still be judged concerning your relationship with Him. Would you let your spouse hold you back from the Lover of your soul? If so, you are saying, in effect, that your spouse is more important to you than God.

If you've stopped going to church because your kids aren't saved or won't attend church, not only are your priorities wrong, but your thinking is also messed up. Without your encouragement, your children will never wind up going to church and you will be farther away from God than before. What sense is there in that?

Some Christians erroneously believe they don't have to attend church. But if you're not associating with other Christians, what are you doing? Do you suppose that a branch of a tree can grow apart from the tree? No, it needs nourishment from the vine and root. It must be connected to the rest of the tree to survive. Believers, too, must be connected to the Body of Christ if they expect to continue in the faith.

Other believers won't come to church because they can't tolerate being told what to do! In reality, they would rather be instructed by the secular mass media and popular culture than by the Word of God and the leadership God has established. What I mean is that many advertisements literally tell you how and where to live, what to wear and eat, and what to do with your time. Ironically, you even pay for all those unsolicited suggestions! Perhaps you've never considered how these things might be dictating the terms of your existence. But the truth is, if the Word of God isn't, they are! It is hard to understand why such people are willing to obey the instructions of the mass media, but become angry at any preacher who tells them what God expects of them! That is what the Bible calls the spirit of this age, the spirit that has blinded the children of disobedience (Eph. 2:2).

If advertisers spend millions of dollars to entice you into buying their products, isn't it a better deal to receive the Word of God free of charge in order to live a glorifying life? That's why pastors exist—to persuade you to make decisions that will have eternal benefits and that will be beneficial to you at the judgement. Pastors encourage you to walk on the straight and narrow road so you can have peace and joy in Christ. If they haven't attempted to influence you, then they have failed in their calling! If you go in and out of church miserable, something is wrong. Pastors should challenge you—and you shouldn't run away from challenges.

Biblically, your first responsibility in life is to love God (Matt. 22:37-38). The second is to love your neighbour (Matt. 22:39). Even the religious lawyer in Luke 10 understood this! The Bible tells us that if we love God, we will do what He says (John 14:15). Why then do people—while claiming to love Him—refuse to obey His Word? It is, perhaps, because Jesus does not occupy the position of greatest importance in their life.

Jesus is our Alpha and Omega (Rev. 22:13), which means He should be our first priority. Our spouse, children, church and work should follow, in that order. Hobbies and recreation should be somewhere at the bottom of the list:

> *For bodily exercise profiteth little: but godliness is profitable unto all things, having promise of the life that now is, and of that which is to come* (1 Tim. 4:8).

God, spouse, children, church, work, recreation. That is the biblical order.

Let's now return to our central Scripture in Luke and read a bit further:

> *And whosoever doth not bear his cross, and come after me, cannot be my disciple. For which of you, intending to build a tower, sitteth not down first, and counteth the cost, whether he have sufficient to finish it? Lest haply, after he hath laid the foundation, and is not able to finish it, all that behold it begin to mock him, Saying, This man began to build, and was not able to finish. Or what king, going to make war against another king, sitteth not down first, and consulteth whether he be able with ten thousand to meet him that cometh against him with twenty thousand? Or else, while the other is yet a great way off, he sendeth an ambassage, and desireth conditions of peace. So likewise, whosoever he be of you that forsaketh not all that he hath, he cannot be my disciple* (Luke 14:27-33).

Essentially, this Scripture instructs us to "count the cost" when we make the decision to follow Jesus. Serving Him should be our major preoccupation for life. It should be a conscious and permanent decision.

I personally believe there are many people in the Church today who were manipulated into the Kingdom of God. Too many didn't believe with their hearts; all they experienced was a mental assent to the gospel. And too many people come to church merely as a ritual. They never experienced salvation, nor do they have a desire to follow the Lord. Yet the Kingdom of God is a relationship that should not be entered into lightly.

Why? Because being born again is not a guarantee against the storms of life. In fact, it may even be an invitation to those storms! After all, the sea of Galilee was calm before the disciples set sail with Jesus (Luke 8:22-23). However, there's nothing that can come against you that God cannot deliver you from. Psalm 34:19 says, *"Many are the afflictions of the righteous: but the Lord delivereth him out of them all."*

The Lord will never leave you at any point in your life, but people will reject and hate you (Luke 6:22). That is part of suffering according to the will of God. It is not a popular thing to be a Christian, but it's what God thinks that really counts.

It doesn't matter what your reputation is in the world. Paul was a leading socialite within his Jewish community, but he counted all things as a loss *"for the excellency of the knowledge of Christ Jesus"* (Phil. 3:8). It doesn't matter how many degrees you have or how rich you are, if Jesus doesn't occupy the position of highest importance in your life, then your priorities are wrong.

And what will happen to those who give up everything to follow Christ? Peter asked Jesus about this very thing:

Then Peter began to say unto him, Lo, we have left all, and have followed thee. And Jesus answered and said,

Verily I say unto you, There is no man that hath left house, or brethren, or sisters, or father, or mother, or wife, or children, or lands, for my sake, and the gospel's, But he shall receive an hundredfold now in this time, houses, and brethren, and sisters, and mothers, and children, and lands, with persecutions; and in the world to come eternal life (Mark 10:28-30).

Does that mean God will give you a hundred houses if you give up yours? Not necessarily. If you owned a hundred houses you probably wouldn't be able to maintain all of them! What I infer from this Scripture is that when you are in the Body of Christ, you become a member of God's family, having many brothers and sisters. And if you go into any of your brethren's families and houses, you are as much welcomed as you would be in your own natural house. That's why preachers can travel around the world and feel comfortable with whomever they lodge.

If you are to be a true disciple of Jesus Christ, you must keep your priorities in line. You must honour God and His Word above everything else in your life and assign things proper values of importance. Discipleship is about commitment, and commitment requires right priorities.

3) Perseverance

The third principle of discipleship is that of perseverance. As believers, God doesn't want us to be quitters in any way. He wants us to endure. He wants us to persevere so that we will see the results of our faith. Galatians 6:9 teaches us that the condition for receiving a harvest is not to faint, but to endure: *"And let us not be weary in well doing: for in due season we shall reap, if we faint not."*

Many times people drop out of the race before the finish line, not realizing that their biggest blessing was just around the corner. Don't shortchange yourself. Hang in there until you see God perform for you what He has promised.

I admire the attitude of the woman who kept knocking on the unjust judge's door, refusing to quit until she had received her request (see Luke 18:1-5). This same attitude can be seen in the man looking for three loaves of bread in Luke 11. They are both portraits of individuals who wouldn't give up. We would do well to imitate their persistent faith.

The woman with the issue of blood faced terrible odds to see Jesus (Mark 5:25-34), as did the ten lepers who came looking to be cleansed (Luke 17:12-19). Still, these societal outcasts persevered until they saw the Master and were able to go away rejoicing. Would they have been healed if they had given up on themselves or their healing?

A disciple must have an abiding faith in His Lord and Master. A disciple must be steadfast and persevere when the storms come. He or she must recognize that God can visit us in a storm (Isa. 29:6), and that the stormy winds may even be a fulfillment of God's will (Ps. 148:8).

4) Fruit Bearing

Another important aspect of discipleship is fruit bearing. John 15:7-8 discusses the importance of fruit bearing in a believer's life:

If ye abide in me, and my words abide in you, ye shall ask what ye will, and it shall be done unto you. Herein is my Father glorified, that ye bear much fruit; so shall ye be my disciples.

In other words, true disciples will be fruit-bearers. Matthew 7:18 tells us that only true disciples can bring forth fruit. They don't hit and miss, but produce more with time. God is well pleased with such individuals.

It is important to understand that before any fruit is ever seen, seed is first planted in the ground. And that seed must *stay* planted, otherwise no fruit would ever come. Psalm 92:12-15 tells us,

> *The righteous shall flourish like the palm tree: he shall grow like a cedar in Lebanon. Those that be planted in the house of the LORD shall flourish in the courts of our God. They shall still bring forth fruit in old age; they shall be fat and flourishing; To shew that the LORD is upright: he is my rock, and there is no unrighteousness in him.*

In other words, if you desire to bear fruit for God, you must first be planted in the house of the Lord (i.e. your local church) and then *stay* there. You will never mature as a disciple in God's Kingdom by moving about from church to church. Instead, obey God's Word and commit to serve your church, family and community. A Christian who isn't planted is blind, and if he tries to disciple another, they will both fall into a ditch (Matt. 15:14). But if you are planted and committed, you will steadily grow into the likeness of your Master (Rom. 8:29).

More About Disciples

Further to the principles we have already touched on, the book of Acts contains some additional revelation about the discipleship process that we can't afford to overlook.

In it we discover that the believers of the early Church engaged in some very specific activities following their conversion. Acts 2:42 summarizes them:

And they continued steadfastly in the apostles' doctrine and fellowship, and in breaking of bread, and in prayers.

The first thing they did was to continue to receive instructions from the apostles (which were really the teachings originally delivered by Jesus). In other words, they *received instruction from the Word of God.* The second thing mentioned in this Scripture is *fellowship.* Acts 2:46 tells us that the early Church met from house to house and developed godly relationships. The third thing they did was to *practice the breaking of bread* (also known as "communion") in remembrance of the death of the Lord Jesus. The final thing was *prayer*, to which I have devoted the final chapter of this book.

The results of applying the practices outlined in Acts 2:42—continuing in the Word, fellowship, the breaking of bread and prayer—can be found in verses 43-47:

And fear came upon every soul: and many wonders and signs were done by the apostles. And all that believed were together, and had all things common; And sold their possessions and goods, and parted them to all men, as every man had need. And they, continuing daily with one accord in the temple, and breaking bread from house to house, did eat their meat with gladness and singleness of heart, Praising God, and having favour with all the people. And the Lord added to the church daily such as should be saved.

Godly fear permeated the city. Miracles were performed in abundance. Benevolence, gladness of heart and praise flowed from the hearts of the believers. And most importantly, a steady flow of unbelievers were coming into the Kingdom of God. What wonderful benefits are to be had by those who commit to a lifestyle of discipleship!

Salvation, you see, is just an inroad to Christianity. After our conversion, God expects us to be instructed and to continue in the Word. That is why He gave ministry gifts to the Church. Apostles, prophets, pastors, teachers and evangelists are to instruct and equip the Body of Christ for the work of the ministry (Eph. 4:12).

Why, you ask, did the early Church devote itself to fellowship? Because lone rangers cannot fulfill the will of God. Neither can hermits. Nobody works alone in God's Kingdom. Even Jesus was made *"like unto His brethren, that He might be a merciful and faithful high priest in things pertaining to God"* (Heb. 2:17).

Through fellowship we also maintain the unity of the Body—which is vital, because Jesus Christ is coming, not for factional denominations, but for His corporate Body.

Communion is significant becaus3e it is a place of fellowship and worship. In communion we discern the body of Christ. The cup of blessing is the blood and the bread is the body (1 Cor. 10:16). As such, we have to recognize the importance of partaking in the communion of the Lord and of examining ourselves (1 Cor. 11:28-29). Many who fail to do so in the Church are weak, sick or dead today (1 Cor. 11:30).

Prayer is also a vitally important element of discipleship. Without prayer, the Church could not continue to exist. It should come as no surprise to us then, that the fifth and final law of expansion is actually a call to prayer.

Six

Strengthen Thy Stakes

"...strengthen thy stakes..." (Isa. 54:2).

The fifth law of expansion is a command to "strengthen thy stakes." Among other things, the Hebrew word translated "strengthen," means to "fasten upon," or "conquer," [3] and is elsewhere translated "cleave," or "be established."

And where do we get strength? It can be from none other than the Lord Himself. *"Finally, my brethren,"* Paul admonishes in Ephesians 6:10, *"be strong in the Lord, and in the power of His might."* Strengthening your stakes, in essence, means to *develop a deeper relationship with God*. One of the main ways this occurs is through prayer, or as Acts 2:42 suggests, through different *kinds* of prayers.

Form & Content

There are many types of prayers, but many Christians have sacrificed content for form. In other words, they have focused more on *how* they are to pray than on *what they are praying.* Consequently, their prayers have become very mechanical. We ought to have a balanced view of prayer so that we don't deny ourselves the effectiveness in prayer God wants us to enjoy. Some Christians determine to pray for an hour each day. So they set their clock and settle down, and then all they do is pray in tongues for a solid hour, hardly stopping to catching their breath. They have already lost the joy and purpose of prayer!

Thank God for the gift of tongues and the ability to pray in tongues. But the purpose of praying in tongues is to build yourself up (Jude 20). It's also an aid for people who do not know what to pray for as they should (Rom. 8:26). The Holy Spirit helps our infirmities or weaknesses and helps us to pray by giving us spiritual diction straight from the heart of God.

But praying is certainly not limited to speaking in tongues. The fourteenth chapter of 1 Corinthians speaks about the importance of praying both in tongues and with our understanding (i.e. in our native language) so that our minds can benefit from what we are praying.

Other Christians come together in what they called a "prayer" meeting, but all they do is groan. They believe that is "travailing." So they travail for hours on end. Yes, Isaiah 66:8 tells us that *"as soon as Zion travailed, she brought forth her children."* Paul the apostle, too, travailed in prayer for the Galatian church (Gal. 4:19).

There is definitely a time for travailing prayer. I once learned that Charles Finney, the renowned evangelist, used to have an intercessor who would go before him to a designated city, rent a hotel room, and pray for the meetings. The man could be heard wailing and travailing for weeks.

Afterward, people would see the hand of God at work in Finney's meetings. Certainly, there is power in groaning, wailing and travailing. In fact, the Holy Spirit Himself intercedes for us *"with groanings which cannot be uttered"* (Rom. 8:26). But we are not to travail in prayer continually.

Allow me to use a natural illustration. A woman travails in childbearing. And, more often than not, after the baby is born, the mother is tired and needs to rest, recover and be strengthened. She needs to refresh her worn-out body. But what would happen if she immediately began travailing again? It would be a waste of time because she is fruitless! The baby has been birthed and there is nothing left for her to deliver. With this illustration in mind, the Body of Christ should take caution that "travailing" doesn't become the kind of vain repetition Jesus instructed us to avoid (Matt. 6:7).

Moreover, a woman must take time to conceive before eventually travailing and delivering a child. In sum, the Church should get the seed of God's Word, nurture it, make it grow and then birth or reproduce it. The book of Ecclesiastes says that there is a time for every activity (Eccl. 3:1). Something is wrong if all that happens in a church prayer meeting is travailing.

There is another problem in prayer I've observed in Christian circles. Some people, endeavoring to make a prayer of petition, write their problems and burdens on a list and go over it, point by point, in prayer. Actually, there is no problem with this system until, over a period of time, it becomes a meaningless mechanical repetition of requests. Our prayer life would be much more fruitful if we would allow the Spirit of God to direct us in prayer.

Prayer is intended to be a form of communion or fellowship with God. Consequently, the manner in which we come into His presence will affect the outcome of our prayers. In other words, we should not be stuck on forms and mechanics. We must endeavour to commune or fellowship with God.

Come with Thanks

Some Christians come to God with only their problems, others with only their complaints and burdens. Many people don't receive answers to their prayers because they pray with the wrong attitude. Would you go to someone's house and start asking for things without first saying "hello" to that person? You probably wouldn't come away with much! The Bible teaches that there is a proper protocol to follow when entering God's presence. King David understood this and wrote about it in Psalm 100:

Make a joyful noise unto the LORD, all ye lands. Serve the LORD with gladness: come before his presence with singing. Know ye that the LORD he is God: it is he that hath made us, and not we ourselves; we are his people, and the sheep of his pasture. Enter into his gates with thanksgiving, and into his courts with praise: be thankful unto him, and bless his name. For the LORD is good; his mercy is everlasting; and his truth endureth to all generations.

David advised that we enter God's presence with *thanksgiving and praise*. That is the Bible way.

Prayer meetings shouldn't be places of misery, you see. On the contrary, they should be places of joy! We should come to the Lord with gladness, singing and shouting. We should come triumphantly, not despairingly. Let's always purpose to come before the Lord with grateful hearts for who He is and for what He has done. Things may not always go the way we would like, but God is still good and He deserves to be acknowledged for His goodness.

Don't be miserable, critical or jealous. Don't be offended at God, preachers, your church, or anyone else for whatever it is you are going through. Have a proper attitude in spite of your problems. God is still the burden-bearer and will give rest to your soul (Matt. 11:29), but you must approach Him respectfully and thankfully:

Are your prayers today mixed with thanksgiving?

Joy & Strength

There is a strong correlation in God's Word between joy and strength. Wherever you see a joyful people you will see a strong people. Whenever you see a weak people you will notice that the ingredient of joy missing. Nehemiah put it this way: *"...the joy of the Lord is your strength"* (Neh. 8:10). If there is joy, then there will be strength. Prayer meetings that lack joy obviously lack strength. That's why the people there are often miserable, empty, downcast and sad. Yet God promised to make us joyful in His house of prayer (Isa. 56:7).

To be joyful means to brighten or cheer up. It means to be happy, merry, or to have a light-hearted disposition.[4] Being happy in God's house of prayer includes all these things. Joyfulness is the opposite of heaviness or gloom. And notice the effect of this joy, described in the same verse above: *"...their burnt offerings and their sacrifices shall be accepted upon mine altar."* A burnt offering is indicative of our total surrender to the Lord. According to the New Testament, our sacrifices are those of thanksgiving and praise (Heb. 13:15), which are to be offered even when our emotions and circumstances are contrary. Our trust and absolute surrender to God's Word and will should override any fleeting feelings we may experience whenever we come to Him.

God wants His people to be joyful in His house of prayer. Why then aren't we joyful? Why is prayer so often done out of a sense of duty and obligation rather than joyfulness? There have been times in my life when I prayed out of a sense of duty because I knew I should do it. But I knew that there was much more to prayer than I was experiencing. Psalm 118:15 says that the voice of rejoicing and salvation is heard in the tabernacles of the righteous. Certainly God will always meet us wherever we are spiritually, but it would be more enjoyable—and fruitful—for us if we purposed to create the kind of atmosphere God desires in prayer.

Psalm 118:15 also tells us that the Lord "doeth valiantly." In other words, He has done great things. When you come before Him, therefore, acknowledge the great things He has done. As an example, listen to the many wonderful things the author of Psalm 118 acknowledges in his song:

> *I called upon the LORD in distress: the LORD answered me, and set me in a large place. The LORD is on my side; I will not fear: what can man do unto me? The LORD taketh my part with them that help me: therefore shall I see my desire upon them that hate me. It is better to trust in the LORD than to put confidence in man. It is*

better to trust in the LORD than to put confidence in princes. All nations compassed me about: but in the name of the LORD will I destroy them. They compassed me about; yea, they compassed me about: but in the name of the LORD I will destroy them. They compassed me about like bees; they are quenched as the fire of thorns: for in the name of the LORD I will destroy them. Thou hast thrust sore at me that I might fall: but the LORD helped me. The LORD is my strength and song, and is become my salvation (Ps. 118:5-14).

Although King David got himself into trouble at various times throughout his life, he continued to acknowledge God's help for all his victories. In Psalm 5:7 he declares,

But as for me, I will come into thy house in the multitude of thy mercy: and in thy fear will I worship toward thy holy temple.

David approached God with a thankful, worshipful heart. We should follow his example if we desire to expand in the things of God.

Worship Him

When the prophets and teachers in the church at Antioch came together, the Bible points out that their first activity was to minister to the Lord (Acts 13:1-2). They devoted themselves to the Lord and worshipped Him. And as they worshipped the Lord, the Holy Spirit spoke to them and gave them divine direction.

The young prophet, Samuel, was also in the habit of ministering to the Lord, even in Eli's dysfunctional home and despite his corrupted priesthood (1 Sam. 2:18). Is it any wonder that God revealed Himself to that little boy?

It is important to note that the first thing Jesus' disciples did after He was taken up from them on the Mount of Olives was to break out in worship:

And he led them out as far as to Bethany, and he lifted up his hands, and blessed them. And it came to pass, while he blessed them, he was parted from them, and carried up into heaven. And they worshipped him, and returned to Jerusalem with great joy: And were continually in the temple, praising and blessing God. Amen (Luke 24:50-53).

Notice that, immediately after they worshipped Jesus, they "returned to Jerusalem with great joy." What is the importance of this statement and the other examples just mentioned? Simply this: if God's house is to be a house of *prayer*, and if God wants to make us *joyful* in His house, then prayer and the worship of God must be closely related, because Luke 24:52 demonstrates that *joy is a by-product of worship*.

When we pray we need to worship God first and foremost—before we do anything else—because an attitude of worship brings you face-to-face with the presence, joy and strength of God. I thank God for who He is. He is the Great Jehovah, the Almighty. He is Jehovah Rapha, the Lord my Healer. He is Jehovah Jireh, the Lord my Provider. He is Jehovah Tsidkenu, the Lord my Righteousness. He is Jehovah Shalom, the Lord my Peace. He is Jehovah Rohi, the Lord my Shepherd. He is Jehovah Shammah, the Lord who is ever present. I begin by thanking God for who He is. We should also worship Him in acknowledgment of all He's done for us. Not a day goes by that I don't thank Him for my salvation and His gift of Christ Jesus.

The disciples worshipped Jesus and returned with great joy to Jerusalem where they were continually in the temple, praising and blessing God. To praise someone means to speak well of that person. In other words, the disciples were speaking well of God. Is it any wonder that God did great things through them? God was able to strengthen their stakes—their relationship with Him— because they worshipped and prayed acceptably.

How About You?

Note that the disciples weren't sulking or murmuring about the fact that their Lord had been taken from them. Neither did they express disappointment about the fact that they had expected Jesus at that time to restore the political kingdom of the Jews. No, they had their eyes and their hearts turned toward heaven where they knew they had a far better and eternal Kingdom—where Christ is still King. Where are your eyes and heart focused today?

The Bible is still true, despite what happened—or didn't happen—to you today. Then why is it you don't seem to receive anything from God when you pray? Understand that the devil is not always to blame. Part of the problem we have, as believers, is that we give too much credit and attention to the devil. Instead, we should examine ourselves and judge our own hearts. Do we do what God commands? Are we walking after the Spirit or are we still engaged in the works of the flesh? The truth is that when the laws of God are working in your life, you probably won't need to worry much about the devil.

Are you praying for a financial breakthrough, but not honouring God with what you presently have? Sometimes we simply need to get our act together and begin to do what the Word says we should be doing so that God's power may flow through us. There are reasons why some prayers aren't answered. The book of James says that if we ask *"amiss"* or with wrong motives, we won't receive what we ask for:

Ye lust, and have not: ye kill, and desire to have, and cannot obtain: ye fight and war, yet ye have not, because ye ask not. Ye ask, and receive not, because ye ask amiss, that ye may consume it upon your lusts (Jas. 4:2-3).

Psalm 66:18 says virtually the same thing: *"If I regard iniquity in my heart, the Lord will not hear me."* What constitutes iniquity in your heart? Bitterness towards a brother or sister, unforgiveness, envy, strife, contention and the like. If you demonstrate any of these behaviours, you can pray all you like, but God cannot hear you. You must first deal with the issues in your heart. Or have you forgotten what Jesus said about bringing an offering to God when there are unresolved offences in your life?

Therefore if thou bring thy gift to the altar, and there rememberest that thy brother hath ought against thee; Leave there thy gift before the altar, and go thy way; first be reconciled to thy brother, and then come and offer thy gift (Matt. 5:23-24).

Beyond your words, what God is looking at is the condition of your heart.

If your purpose in giving to God is to become a millionaire, then you have an impure motive. You will also probably never become a millionaire because God cannot entrust wealth to the greedy. Giving to God should be a form of worship. If you can adopt the proper attitude in your giving, and understand that God is able to multiply your seed so you can do more for Him next time, then you are on a roll.

What is your motive in asking God to do something? What is the pastor's motive for having a bigger church and a larger congregation? Is it to reach the lost and dying or to increase tithes and offerings?

You can't expect to receive the blessings of the Lord with iniquity in your heart. It doesn't work that way. Just be honest with yourself and rectify your ways. You can't pull the wool over God's eyes. He knows everything already, and He knows where your affections lie.

Furthermore, don't try to pray with elevated, religious language, thinking that it will impress Him. It doesn't matter how much "thous," "thys," and "thees" you can appropriately use; faith is the only thing that moves God (Heb. 11:6). Do not pretend in His presence; He knows your capabilities already. Don't parrot anyone in prayer because God is no respecter of persons. He made everyone unique. Talk to God from your own heart, with your own words. The Bible tells us that God spoke with Moses as a man would speak with his friend (Exod. 33:11). God wants intimate, unfeigned communication with you, as well.

God longs for worshippers (John 4:23). It doesn't matter what posture you assume, just let your heart and mind be with Him. Sometimes I walk around when I pray. Sometimes I sit, and sometimes I kneel. I don't get into any pattern. I don't try to mechanize the presence of God.

God isn't against your prayer request list, but worship Him first and relax in His presence. You'll still have time to get to your list. And even if you don't, He knows what you've written, anyway!

They Worshipped Him

We have already established that worship should precede our prayers. This is especially true with regard to our *requests* of God. Notice the pattern laid out in Matthew 8:2-3:

And, behold, there came a leper and worshipped him, saying, Lord, if thou wilt, thou canst make me clean. And Jesus put forth his hand, and touched him, saying, I will; be thou clean. And immediately his leprosy was cleansed.

The leper first worshipped Him before saying anything. Then, he made his request of Jesus, and Jesus immediately healed him. This same pattern can be found in the very next chapter:

While he spake these things unto them, behold, there came a certain ruler, and worshipped him, saying, My daughter is even now dead: but come and lay thy hand upon her, and she shall live. And Jesus arose, and followed him, and so did his disciples… But when the people were put forth, he went in, and took her by the hand, and the maid arose. And the fame hereof went abroad into all that land (Matt. 9:18-19, 25-26).

The ruler first worshipped, then made his request. Jesus then granted it. Matthew 15:22-28 contains the

account of the Syrophenicia
for her daughter. She also ᵛ

In all of these examp
Jesus received their petiti
prised that sometimes iɾ
manifested in people's
There are many examp
occurring after worsh
34). Even the final instructions ɟ
came after they had worshipped Him (se
16-20). Worship is an important key to answered praye

Summary

We could quickly recap the points made in this chapter as follows: The strength we are looking for is the joy of the Lord (Neh. 8:10), which is given in His house of prayer (Isa. 56:7). And effective prayer is always preceded by worship of the Most High. That is how your stakes are strengthened and how you place yourself in position for expansion.

Time to Expand

You will recall that the purpose of this book has been to help you expand in the things of God. Defined simply, *expansion is practically living in everything God has prepared for you*. Expansion is about not being limited to any person, thing or place, but possessing the ability to do and be everything God calls upon you to do and be. God's desire is to increase you—to transform you from glory to glory. With God there is no barrenness. There is no problem, limitation or circumstance that can dictate your outcome if

...o fulfill God's requirements for a fruitful ...it another day. Take God at His Word today ...m to expand you in your home, church, com- ...d nation to bring glory to His name. Put God's ...xpansion to work and start expanding—today!

An Important Message

If you have never met Jesus Christ and received God's forgiveness, you can know Him today. God cares for you and wants to help you in every area of your life. That is why He sent Jesus to die for you. Jesus paid the price for all the wrong things you have ever done and offers you a new start in life. You can find peace with God this very moment and know for certain that you will go to heaven when you die by choosing to accept what Jesus has done for you, and by turning your life over to Him. Take some time to think about this decision. It is the most important decision you will ever make. To accept God's forgiveness, all you need to do is ask. If you're not sure what to say, simply use the following prayer:

> *God, I ask you to forgive me of my sins. I believe You sent Jesus to die on the cross for me. I receive Jesus Christ as my personal Saviour. I declare Him to be the Master of my life and I give my life to Him. Thank You, Lord, for saving me, and for making me new. In Jesus' Name, Amen.*

If you prayed that prayer and meant it from your heart, I welcome you into the family of God! Please let us know about your decision by letter or E-mail, using the contact information found at the back of this book. We will be happy to send you some free informational materials to help you get started in your new life with Jesus.

For now, simply start to read the Bible a little bit each day, starting with the New Testament. Talk to God about your life and ask for His help every day. Ask God to help you find a Bible-believing church where you can get to know other Christians and be taught life-changing truths from God's Instruction Manual—the Bible.

We look forward to hearing from you!

In Christ's love,

Richard Ciaramitaro

Endnotes

[1] *New Concise Webster's Dictionary*, 1984 ed., "Expand."

[2] James Strong, *The New Strong's Concordance of the Bible* (Nashville: Thomas Nelson Publishers, 1990), "Greek Dictionary of the New Testament," p. 45, entry # 3100.

[3] Strong, *Hebrew and Chaldee Dictionary*, p. 38, entry # 2388.

[4] This series of definitions derived from Strong's *Hebrew and Chaldee Dictionary*, p. 118, entry # 8055.

Other Ministry Resources

by Richard Ciaramitaro

Audio Cassette Series

Title	$ Cdn.	$ US	# in Series
Capacity	15.00	9.00	4
Commandments	12.00	7.25	3
Confidence	15.00	9.00	4
Controlling Your Appetite	12.00	7.25	3
Creating a Spiritual Atmosphere	12.00	7.25	3
Enthusiasm	15.00	9.00	4
Laws of Expansion	15.00	9.00	4
Laws of Release	15.00	9.00	4
Moving On to Great Faith	25.00	15.00	7
Passion	18.00	10.75	5
Prerequisites For Warfare	15.00	9.00	4
Reaching Your Potential	21.00	12.50	6
Righteousness	30.00	18.00	9
The Power Twins of Hell (Comparison & Competition)	12.00	7.25	3
Zealous of Good Works	25.00	15.00	7

To order a tape series please fill out the order form on the following page. Please **add $1.00 per tape** in each tape series for **shipping & handling**. Allow 2-4 weeks for delivery.

Books

Laws of Expansion	8.25	5.00
Moving On to Great Faith	8.25	5.00

To order a book please fill out the order form on the following page. Please **add $1.50 per book** for **shipping & handling**. Allow 2-4 weeks for delivery.

Order Form

To order ministry materials, simply fill out the appropriate information below and mail or fax this form to the address at the bottom of this page. Be sure to use the US price list when ordering from the US or abroad.

Title	**Quantity**	**Price**	**Total**

Shipping and Handling $_____

Total Price of Order: $_____

Shipping Information

Name: _____

Street: _____

City: _____

State/Province:_____Country: _____

Postal/Zip Code: _____

Phone: (   ) _____

Payment Information

___ Cheque   ___Visa   ___ Master Card   ___ American Express

Credit Card Number: _____

Expiry Date: _____

Cardholder's Name: _____

Signature of Cardholder: _____

(continued on next page)

Cheques may be made payable to:

Windsor Christian Fellowship

Please mail or fax your order to:

Windsor Christian Fellowship
4490 - 7th Concession
Windsor, Ontario, Canada   N9A 6J3
Fax: *(519) 972-8915*   Phone: *(519) 972-5977*